I0455492

In God We Trust – Because We Sure Can't Trust Congress!

By

Haywood Roberts

"In all those things which deal with people, be liberal, be human. In all those things which deal with the people's money, or their economy, or their form of government be conservative."

Dwight D. Eisenhower

Table of Contents

Preface by D.B.C.

Introduction

Chapters

Preface

You all remember me – well at least those of you who are a bit older –I'm the guy that invented airplane hijacking. No, not the terrorist kind, that came later. In my case when I jumped from the tail of that Boeing 727 back in 1971 with a suitcase full of cash, everyone marveled at my audacious scheme.

Well, the truth is that I was just creating my own personal IRA (Individual Retirement Account) before Congress ever dreamed it up. Only mine worked! For some reason I just didn't trust those guys in Washington to look after my future.

Of course, I could have lived a simpler (and some out say saner) life – working 9 to 5, paying my taxes every April 15th and trying to keep up with all the incomprehensible laws spewing out of Washington every session of Congress. But, after years of trying to anticipate, adjust and just plain survive, one day the "tilt" light went on in my mental pinball game – and the game was over. My circuits overloaded!

So I dumped my Wall Street Journal, my Kiplinger Washington Letter and my U.S. News and World Report along with other assorted guides to the Washington scene from my briefcase and had it filled with cold, hard cash---and I jumped.

I don't recommend my solution to everyone. Crazy schemes like mine usually work only once. Maybe this book will help you understand and come to your terms with how to deal with the madhouse on the Potomac.

From the Friendly Sky

D.B.C.

Introduction

It is always hard to find the right title for a book. You want something that catches a reader's attention – maybe even rivets them. It has to peak their interest and make someone want to read what is inside (or perhaps selfishly, wants to make them want to buy the book!).

Addressing this subject, I thought about (and then rejected) the title, "Jaws III – It Still Isn't Safe To Go Into The Water." After all, why blame the poor shark for what happens in Washington – they are just doing what comes naturally. They would have to be trained for years to be as sharp toothed as the average Congressperson. After all when a Senator or Representative shows their teeth it is usually only for the TV camera.

Another title that came to mind was, "Mr. Smith Goes To Washington—No Wonder He Chose A Motel Register Name." But with all the sex scandals in Washington I didn't want to play on the foibles and petty cheating that goes on – that is chicken feed stuff anyway compared to the real skullduggery. After all, you don't want to focus on the sideshow and miss the two ring circus in the main tent.

Finally, I rejected the title, "Mafia in Government, Legalized Number Running." This too just didn't fit.   After all, you might even have a chance of winning a mafia run numbers game.   With Congress, you pay your money and know you will lose! In fact, it is the only gambling game I know of where you place your bet and hope that your bet is all that you will lose.

Now if you think that I am somewhat cynical about our present Congress let me set the record straight. I am not cynical, I am just plain mad. We have a system that is not working very well for the vast majority of Americans, is self-perpetuating and is a clear and present danger to us all. And it is about time we woke up and started to clean house…Senate too for that matter.

If you are Super Rich (say a net worth of $20 million or more) or poor, then this book is probably not for you. The present system really works pretty well for you. If you are between, then you need to know about how the system really works.   Only armed with knowledge is there hope for you to cope with the hottest TV show of the 21st Century… "Life with Congress."

One thing you need to know from the start. Your average Congressperson be they Senator or Representative, is usually a pretty nice person. In fact the campaign mechanism forces them to be friendly as speckled pups. Oh, some of these dogs are friendlier than others, some behave better than others, but they all wag their tails when they see you.

Most are victims of the system too. Individually they can make all the sense in the world, have all the best of intentions. Let them become part of the Congressional Pack and you should gather the family and hold tight to your wallet. That is part of the problem. How do you get rid of that cute, cuddly puppy that always wags its tail for you and licks your hand and sleeps quietly at your feet? He (or she) isn't to blame; it is all those other guys and gals, in someone else's district, that caused the whole problem.

Enough of the preliminaries. First let me tell you a story, about leprechauns.

Chapter 1 Leprechauns and other tall tales!

In the cornfields of Nebraska there are many people of Irish descent. Their grandparents and great grandparents came to work on the intercontinental railroad in the middle of the 19th Century. After their part in that great adventure was finished they stayed to farm and work the rich Nebraska soil and raise cattle, corn and families.

Among these adventurers was a red headed Irishman named Timothy O'Reilly. Small framed, but powerful, he was also a careful man. All his wages from the railroad he kept in gold, buried deep beneath a large rock outcrop on a spot of land he had bought with the first of his savings.

One evening, in early 1872 Timothy was putting his week's wages in this cache when a small figure appeared out of the corner of his eye. He could scarcely believe it – but there was not a doubt in his mind that this diminutive creature was in fact a leprechaun!

Timothy had never seen one before, though he had heard of them for nearly all his life from his mother and sisters. They had told him much of the mystical powers of this leprechaun.

"Top of the day to you, Mr. O'Reilly," said the soft spoken leprechaun. "My name is Usa."

"And what be you doing Mr. O'Reilly? Ahh! I see you have a hiding place for your gold. Very wise indeed!" said Usa, with a twinkle in his eye.

"In fact it is about your gold that I have come to see you." Usa said smiling. "I'm sure" he continued, "you know that leprechauns can be trusted in such matters." He winked wryly at Timothy.

Timothy was mighty uneasy, but he was also very curious about just what Usa had in mind. He continued to listen as he leaned back against the outcrop.

"You don't really trust me. I can see that, and there is no reason in the world why you should. But, let me tell you what we propose. We are in need of additional gold for our…um..special work. I am authorized to borrow some of your gold with a promise to return it next month, plus $1/10^{th}$ extra for your trouble. Each month you can decide how much or how little of your gold you would like to let me have and we will settle up at month's end." Usa fell silent to let Timothy think about what he had proposed.

Timothy thought a long while. He didn't lie to part with any of his hard earned gold. But $1/10^{th}$ more! Boy, could he put that to good use.

In the end he gave Usa ten gold dollars, as a test. The whole month he stewed and worried, had he been tricked? Could he really trust a leprechaun? But, at the end of the month. Usa returned with eleven gold dollars, the original ten and the extra $1/10^{th}$ he had promised.

Timothy was very happy with Usa and his arrangement. Each month he gave Usa a little more of his gold. And his savings hoard grew and grew.

After six months, Usa suggested to Timothy that rather than trade gold once a month, if Timothy wanted him to Usa would keep a record book with all Timothy's gold recorded in dollars and the fees for Usa using them. Timothy could have his money any time he wanted and for this service, since it was easier for Usa too, Usa would add another $1/5^{th}$ to the fee. Timothy was delighted with the extra fee and frankly he was tired of carrying the gold to and from the cache each month. Also he was always concerned that someone would follow him or stumble onto his cache. This seemed much safer. What's more, Usa had always settled up faithfully and Timothy had grown to have great trust in him.

At the end of the year, Timothy reviewed his records and found that the one thousand dollars he started the year with was now worth two thousand dollars thanks to Usa. He was very happy indeed!

11

Once each year Timothy made the long trip to town from the railroad camp. He enjoyed the trip, using it to settle accounts, buy some necessities and pay his taxes. This year Timothy settled up with Usa and Usa paid him the full two thousand dollars.

When he arrived in Junction City, Timothy called on his bookkeeper and told him of his good fortune (without details of course). Being an honest man, Timothy wanted to pay what he owed. His bookkeeper told him that a new territorial tax required the payment of 25% of his interest earnings for the year, or $250 in tax. Timothy was annoyed to pay the tax but was still happy as he left with $1750 to spend.

At least he was happy until he stopped at the General Store to buy the things he needed. He noticed in the window that the new rifle he wanted was now $50. Last year he remembered it was only $25. In fact, he soon found that almost everything that he wanted was twice as much as it had been a year before.

Timothy was really angry when he found that his gold coins were now worth twice what they were worth a year before but that now he was actually worse off after paying his taxes. And his bookkeeper told him that the result would have been the same had he kept the coins and cashed them in because the new territorial tax covered appreciation when you cashed in – something he called capital gains. Even though in terms of what those gold dollars would buy there was no real "gain."

Whether Usa intended to cheat him Timothy didn't know. He knew that the result was clear enough, Timothy ended the year less well off than when he started.

The moral of the story is… Don't trust a leprechaun with your gold…especially if his name is U.S.A.

In case you think that such leprechauns don't exist I have some news for you. Consider your FDIC insured bank account on which you are paid say 2% interest. Let's say you deposit $1000 at the start of the year, just like Timothy, and at the end of the year your $1000 is worth $1020. So far so good. But then there are taxes to consider. Let's say income tax only takes 25%. That leaves you with $1015. But the Federal Reserve thinks that a 2% annual inflation rates is great (about that more later) and so you would need the full $1020 just to buy the same items you would have bought a year before with $1000. But after taxes you only have $1015. And over a period of several years this gets worse and worse. That 2% inflation rate in 25 years will erode more than half your buying power when you started, and that assumes only 2% inflation.

And they wonder why Americans don't save more. With leprechauns like these yet! But then your deposit was insured by …guess who? U.S.A. Always looking after your best interest of course.

So much for fairy tales. Let's get to the real gold diggers…

Chapter 2 Gamesmanship. These are the rules…but only for today!

Playing by the Rules – Their Rules that is!

How many of us would play a game where at any time one of the players could change the rules to suit themselves? And what if they could not only change the rules for future play but could change the rules for that part of the game that has already been played? I doubt many of us would be interested in playing such a game.

Yet that is exactly what is happening, with disturbing and increasing frequency, in the Congress of the United States.

Imagined you are playing blackjack (or 21 if you like) and after two hours you are ahead by $50. Just then the dealer announces that the house wins unless the players have exactly 21 in their hands each play. Furthermore, the change affects anyone playing…retroactively. Now, he says you owe the house $50 rather than the other way around.

In the words of Ollie North, that is a really "neat idea."

No way you say. Couldn't happen. I agree, not in Las Vegas or in Reno or in Atlantic City. But in Washington DC, in that great casino on the

Potomac? You bet it can happen…any session of Congress.

An Example or Two

Just for starters let's look at what Congress did back in the 1986 Tax Reform Act to capital gains, adding to it what they did in the middle 1970's to Social Security.

Start with the case of Mr. and Mrs. Smith, a retired couple age 70. The Smiths back in the 1940's and 1950's invested their savings in stock of IBM, DuPont, General Motors and ATT as well as in a mutual fund, Dreyfus. Their investments at their cost totaled $45,000. Over the years, even after the great crash of 1987, their investment nest-egg had grown to $450,000. From their investments the Smiths have an annual dividend and interest income of $20,000. In addition, Dreyfus pays them a capital gains distribution averaging $20,000 a year. They also have Social Security, having paid into the system from the beginning, equal to $12,000 a year.

Back before the Social Security "reform" in the middle 1970's and before the Tax "Reform" Act of 1986 Mr. and Mrs. Smith would have paid tax in 1986 as follows:

Income Item	Total Income	Table Income	Federal Tax
Social Security	12,000	0	
Dividend/Interest	20,000	20,000	
Capital Gains	20,000	8,000	
Totals	52,000	28,000	3,107

Now, after these wonderful "reforms" Mr. and Mrs. Smith have a tax picture that looks like this.

Interest Item	Total Income	Taxable Income	Federal Tax
Social Security	12,000	6,000	
Dividend/Interest	20,000	20,000	
Capital Gains	20,000	20,000	
Totals	52,000	46,000	7,276

In other words, the Smith in 1987 saw their taxable income increased by 65% while their total tax bill just for the Federal government increased by a whopping 134%. Now in later years there were changes that both increased and decreased this tax bite. On Social Security instead of being taxable up to 50% it is now taxable up to 85%. And dividends and capital gains are taxed at lesser rates if you are under the 15% tax bracket but higher as your taxable income increases.

Back to the Smiths in the late 1980's. They have even more unpleasant surprises awaiting them if they decide that they need to change their investments. Let's say the Smiths feel that IBM and General Motors are no longer the investments they should have at their age. They would like more present income. So in early 1991 having been scared by the roller coaster markets in 1987 and 1990 due to the crash of the stock market in November 1987 and later the Gulf War, they sell their investments in IBM and General Motors realizing a gain for tax purposes of $100,000. Notice I did not say they realized a profit of $100,000 but a "gain" for tax purposes. We will discuss the difference a little later. For now let's look at the tax effect of the sale the Smith made, comparing the tax effect before and after the Social Security and Tax Act "reforms."

	Taxable Income	Added Tax in 1991	Net After Tax
Pre Reform	40,000	12,854	87,147
Post Reform	100,000	33,000	67,000
Net Change	+60,000	+20,146	-20,146

The effect on the Smiths was that they now needed to find an alternative investment yielding at least 50% more than their previous investment just to break even on an after tax basis. The real effect is that they are, as a practical matter, locked in to their investments without regard to the underlying value of their investments.

Now how can this be? I remember all the hoopla when they passed the 1986 Tax Act. All the commentators said that capital gains were going to go up from 25% to 28%, an increase of only 3%. Well that is all very true if you are talking about the Super Rich who were paying the very top rate. For the average American taxpayer with a little capital gains on their nest-egg the tax increase was considerably more substantial. The effect for Mr. and Mrs. Smith was a 150% plus increase in their effective capital gains tax.

Now, hold on just a minute. The Smiths could have sold their stock in 1986 and avoided the new capital gains tax on their old gains. That is certainly true enough. But let's consider a couple of additional items.

First, to avoid this tax the Smiths would have had to incur commissions to get out and back into the market. Even if they used a discount broker these would have been significant. Second, you are assuming a level of sophistication on the part of the 70 year old Smiths that may not apply to the average senior citizen in their position. Third, they had another factor to consider. On their death any capital gains would not be taxed under current law and the only tax would be the estate tax. Based on the assets we have assumed there would have been little or no estate tax. It is reasonable to assume that the Smiths would want to pass on to their children as much of what they had accumulated as they could. So for them to have paid almost $100,000 in capital gains tax, which on their death would have been stepped up in basis and not taxed, is not a logical choice. In summary it would not have been the best choice for the Smiths to have sold in 1986 to avoid the increased rates.

Worst of all for the Smiths is the fact that there was no real profit to be taxed to begin with! Remember earlier when I said that they had realized a "gain for tax purposes but had not realized a "profit?" Here is what I meant. Since 1940 inflation in the United States had by 1986 increased prices roughly 10 fold. In other words the Coca Cola that cost 5 cents in 1940 was now in 1986 selling for 50 cents. And yes today in 2016 it is over $1. The house that sold for $10,000 in 1940 sold for $100,000 in 1986. The car that cost $950 in 1940 sold for $9,500 in 1985 and now sells for well over $20,000 in 2016. And we will not even talk about the old penny postcard.

Stocks that were worth $45,000 in the 1940's and in 1986 were worth $450,000 in terms of what they will buy had not appreciated a penny. So when the

Smiths sold their stock they only got back (in terms of what the price of their stock would buy in real goods and services) only what they invested. There was no real economic profit, only what the tax man calls "taxable gain." If they sold all their investments they would have had left, after taxes, only about $325,000 which means that for every $1 they invested they got back only 72 cents.

Remember those pesky leprechauns you probably did not believe in?

The same results occur whether the assets you own are stocks, bonds, real estate or your own business. Yes, since 1986 there have been more changes in the tax laws, some helpful (such as no tax on certain dividends and capital gains held long term for those in lowest tax brackets) but the fact remains that any session of Congress they may change the rules on you. At times this can actually benefit you such as after the financial crisis of 2008 they allowed those having to take required minimum distributions from their IRA's to not have to make that withdrawal. But most of the time the changes are not that favorable.

So for Mr. and Mrs. Smith in 1987 these were the rewards from a grateful Congress, for your years of hard work, living through the Great Depression, fighting two world wars, a police action in Korea, Vietnam and the Persian Gulf and for savings and

21

investing in American. Your Congress thanks you for your most generous contribution – one of course you never knew you made!

By the way, who do you think gave you all this inflation in the first place? Who ran the printing presses that over inflated the currency? Who spent the money that they didn't have? You guessed it, that old leprechaun, Usa!

A few years ago something similar happened in California with property taxes. For a variety of reasons property prices skyrocketed and so did property taxes. Did the California legislature help the people? Hell no! It took a courageous group of citizens to push through a proposition amending their state constitution to redress the evils of property taxes that threatened to drive millions of Californians from homes on which they no longer could pay the taxes. You should have heard the bureaucrats scream!

And more recently in Nebraska and elsewhere in the corn belt high commodity prices (which have since collapsed) drove up the value of farm land. Again, did the legislators reduce taxes? Nope, they just raked in the windfall. When prices were going up everyone was happy but when the music stopped that was another story entirely.

Congress is a little smarter. They take only small bites from small parts of the electorate at a time. Being careful to hide as many of these as possible. Only later do those affected find out what has really happened to them. Usually too late to do anything about it. Can you really blame special interest groups for having lobbying efforts constantly monitoring and massaging what is going on that affects them. Sadly the vast public has no such lobby.

So you probably think this is the end of the tale of woe for Mr. and Mrs. Smith? I hope you are right but our Congressional gamesmen and women are still at work. Having snookered the Smiths into not cashing in under the old rates with the lure of no capital gains at death, they are now considering once again a tax on capital gains at death. Forgetting their last experience with this when they had to repeal the law that created a nightmare for accountants and their clients who could not in many cases find the basis of the stocks to be valued. But that is not Congresses problem, right? And had the 1989 Catastrophic Medical Plan been allowed to stand that would have added 15% immediately and 25% by 1993 to their tax bill for good measure. And Obamacare may well add to that tax burden depending on their income levels, income levels they are clever enough NOT to link to inflation just like they did not link the income levels for taxing Social Security to inflation, or the AMT

(Alternative Minimum Tax) and a host of other sneaky tax increases resulting from over inflation. Told you these leprechauns were clever little devils!

To put the icing on the cake the most insidious new idea in Washington is the "need based entitlement" which is a neat little phrase by which they plan to steal (opps sorry to have used the real word), by which they plan to redress past mistakes (that is more PC) by deciding that the Smiths are just too rich and they don't need Social Security or Medicare, at least not until Congress has stripped them of all their assets. More about that later.

Social (In)Security and the Tax Reform Act – Part II

With the perspective of how the Social Security and Tax Reform Acts work in the real world it is time to consider how such horrible results could occur

Social Security Reform = 1970 Style

In the middle 1970's Congress woke up to the fact that the Johnson, Great Society give away years and the Vietnam War had combined to result in the worst inflationary spiral in the last century, starting with a gut-wrenching spiral of oil prices. In 2016 with falling oil prices it is hard to remember sitting in line at gas stations to pay high prices just to get a few gallons of gasoline but it happened. And prices jumped just as they have recently plunged.

Looking out to the year 2010 and beyond it was obvious (even to Congress) that Social Security would be dead broke unless steps were taken to "fix" the system. In 2010 the baby boomers of WWII would be ready to retire and the money wouldn't be there. So the first step in the "fix" was a massive increase in social security taxes, doubling and tripling the effective tax at the upper end in a few short years.

To sell that one to the baby boomers Congress decided that those in retirement would have to sacrifice as well. As would the surviving spouses and children of deceased workers.

Step one was to take away benefits only a few realized they had. So they eliminated survivor benefits for wives and children of deceased workers after age 18. No longer would full time college students qualify to continue to receive benefits. Sorry kids if your deceased parent counted on that. Tough luck. So for a worker who had planned his or her life insurance needs based on survivor benefits from Social Security and whom either could not, at an order age, get or afford increased coverage it was just too bad. After all, someone has to sacrifice for past Congressional mistakes. And you can bet it will not be your local Congress person!

Welcome to the blackjack table- Washington style!

But widows and orphans were not the only easy pickens. Best of all were those golden gooses – the golden agers. Congress decided that another really neat idea would be to change the rules on the taxation of Social Security benefits.

Up to this point Social Security benefits from the beginning had not been treated as taxable income. Now they decided that if you were retired and had an income over $25,000 (if single) or $32,000 (if married) that you deserved to be taxed on one half your social security benefit. The theory (and they always have a nice sounding theory while they are picking your pocket) was that since one half your social security was never taxed when it was paid in it is only fair it be taxed now.

Did they ever stop to think about those who had retired and who had relied on the rules then in effect? Those who now having given up their jobs cannot go back and say to their employers "Gosh, if I had known this I would have waited to retire, can I have my old job back?" Or, those who counting on their after-tax income had purchased their retirement homes or made commitments for their retirement? Hell no! They just saw a golden goose ripe for the plucking and they plucked right away.

26

Lest you think the story is fully told later Congress decided to tax up to 85% of Social Security and this time they did not even bother with an excuse to cover up stealing this money. And of course that old leprechaun Usa is still with us since they did not index the income levels for inflation. So as inflation lessens the value of your dollars it pushes more and more people over the limits for paying tax on their Social Security. And is there a doubt they plan to eliminate it all together using their "need based" standard? One way to eliminate income inequality of course is to make sure everyone is poor, other than those in the beltway and their special friends and contributors of course. And guess who will set the rules that determine if you are needy enough to get back some of the money that you paid into the system and on which you paid both a Social Security and income tax? Right again, old Usa!

They have a dandy game plan set out. First they plan to engage in a little old fashioned class warfare attacking the top 1% of earners and income inequality. Hey they plan, and indeed have already started, a generational war. Set the juniors against their parents and grandparents. After all, who deserves it more those who saved and worked for it or their children and grandchildren who have to pay the taxes today. Of course junior you realize that when your turn comes they will have gotten yours too! The burden of the current Social Security tax is enormous on the young. They have a right to feel burdened. But let's blame the right folks for the burden. It isn't the seniors; it's the Senators…and Representatives.

Tax Reform –
Now You See It – Now You Don't!

Probably one of the biggest bill of goods ever sold to the American people was the Tax Reform Act of 1986. In one fell swoop Congress changed practically every rule in the book. They left many a citizen out on a limb and then proceeded to saw it off. A good many bankruptcies could be traced back to the Tax Reform Act of 1986 and the damage continues to this day. When a dispassionate study is done years down the road on the Savings and Loan, Insurance and Banking crisis that has ebbed and flowed since the 1980's and continues as we approach 2020 a great deal of the credit may well be given to the Tax Reform Act. The depressing effect on real estate prices starting with the Savings and Loan crisis pushed a serious problem into a catastrophe which only escalated later in the collapse of Lehman Brothers and the resulting real estate and financial collapse of 2008 whose effects linger still.

One of my personal favorite "neat ideas" in the 1986 Tax Reform Act was the effective elimination of the IRA or Individual Retirement Account. After the 1970's it was obvious to most of the baby boomers that there was little chance they would ever see a dime out of Social Security despite all the talk about fixing the system. So when the IRA was created it seemed like a way for many Americans to really have a chance to save for their retirement and to do so with real, after tax, dollars not those phony inflation eaten, highly taxed current earning dollars. But guess what? It worked too well! People really started using IRA's. So what did Congress do? They changed the rules in mid-game and eliminated the IRA for those people who needed it most for their retirement, the middle class. They left it in place for those people who had proved that they couldn't or wouldn't use the IRA. And if the remaining group ever does starting using it do I have any bets they will not take away the benefit of the IRA for them too? I didn't think so.

Another "neat idea" was a real beauty. Business had been encouraged since the Kennedy years to invest in new plant and equipment by qualifying for an investment tax credit. In the 1986 Tax Reform Act they decided to do away with the investment credit. Did they make the elimination apply to equipment purchased in the future? Of course but in addition they reached back all the way to the first of January 1986 (some six months before the Tax Reform Act was even under serious consideration) and eliminated the investment credit for any equipment purchased anytime in 1986.

How would you liked to have been the business that in early 1986 bought equipment based on the rules then in effect. Who calculated what you could pay based on the after tax cost only to find that after it was too late to do anything about it the rules were changed on you. What do you expect, an even break? Better luck next time.

Of course the real biggie was capital gains. All those investors who had bought stocks, bonds, real estate or other assets based on the tax rules in effect when they bought then, rules that had been in effect almost from the beginning of income tax in the United States were the really big losers under Tax Reform.

The average investor will find that their effective tax under Tax Reform has doubled or even tripled on their capital gain investment income. Because the tax laws had encouraged this investment, and the reliance on the existing method of taxation was reasonable, carried no weight with a Congress bent on "Tax Reform"

The list of losers under Tax Reform is a long one, from real estate investors (and the banks, insurance companies and those infamous savings and loans that loaned on real estate) to stock investors and charities. Many who thought they were winners had just not read the rules yet. And they had best read them quickly, before they change again.

The Art of Planning in America

In recent years we have heard a great deal about financial planning. It seems as though just about everyone who used to be a salesperson (whether of life insurance or mutual funds or stocks) is now a "Financial Planner."

Well, the truth is that until Congress stops changing the rules in the middle of the game, welshing on promises made to the American people, reneging on its debts and begins exercising a modicum of self-restraint no one can plan more than a few months in advance.

The effects of this are yet to be fully felt but it is almost certain to result in only the shortest of timeframe planning both by individuals and businesses. No one in their right mind would make a major commitment relying on the rules presently in effect. Congress has proved repeatedly that they will tear up the rule book any time they choose.

Social Security and income tax are only two examples. They are, however, examples that affect nearly everyone. Get away from those affected generally and Congress is even more willing to reverse course on anyone unsuspecting enough to play the game by their rules.

For example, they now have their knives out for all sorts of so-called "entitlement" programs. One of these (or at least it was before our recent terrorist wars) was military pensions. I may agree that military pensions are generous, perhaps too generous. But I think when you have lured men and women in to the Armed Forces, persuaded them to give up civilian employment for the hazards and family hardships that are part of a military career and have promised them in return a generous retirement you don't change the rules simply because you don't like the game anymore. For future inductees and recruits, fine. Those who have served faithfully and well deserve far better treatment.

Compare how Congress behaves with a businessman for just a moment. Jake owns his own hardware store. For twenty years Mildred was his hard working assistant. Jake promised Mildred if she stayed with him that he would pay her a pension for the rest of her life. This year Jake made some stupid mistakes. He over ordered some inventory, got carried away in an expansion and bought a piece of equipment that turned out to be worthless. Jake called Mildred and told her that under the circumstances he could no longer afford to pay her the full pension and would have to cut it back by one third. Can you imagine the outcry from Mildred? Can you see a court letting Jake off the hook on his promise? But Congress does exactly this, time and time again. And it gets away with it!

Under the Constitution of the United States we are protected against retroactive laws as they affect criminal behavior. The Constitution prohibits what are called *ex poste facto* laws. Back in the days of good old King George III they thought it a "neat idea" too to pass laws after the fact. The king would wait until one of his subjects would take an action that was legal at the time and then make it illegal retroactively, often at the price of the subject's head. Our founding fathers had quite enough of that bit of sport, among other things, and stopped the practice in the United States once and for all.

It is high time that we extended the Constitutional prohibition to civil laws as well and protect those who have reasonably relied on the laws of the land in conducting their affairs.

One, Two, Three Strikes and You're Out in the Old Ball Game!

Thinking about this subject reminded me of when I was a boy growing up in the southeastern part of Missouri. I lived in a small lead mining town of Bonne Terre where there was no organized little league. In fact we were lucky to find five or six kids our age to play ball. Our brand of baseball was a pick-up game after school or on a Saturday. You would round up a few friends and find an open field and play as best you could.

There weren't any fixed rules for these games. The rules changed to fit the number of players, size of the field and height of the grass. Usually the guy who brought the ball made the rules.

Many a game broke up with a fight over the rules and the fight was usually settled by the guy with the ball picking it up and heading home.

I guess these fellows grew up to become Congressmen. Just like back then, when the middle of the game they are behind, or they just don't like how the game is going, they just pick up their ball and leave. Only now it is more likely that it is *our* ball that they have picked up and taken home.

Chapter 3 The Super Rich get richer, the poor do ok, and those in the muddle (new word for middle) pays the bill.

Secrets Of The Really Rich

Someone once said that the rich are different. They probably are. But let's define what we mean by "rich." The folks I am talking about are those on the Forbes 400 list and those who don't make the list but have at least $20 million in net worth. In the 21st Century progressive liberals came up with a neat new catch phrase for that, the top 1%. And what in the Great Depression people called millionaires due to inflation are now billionaires. Can trillionaires be far ahead? Being a millionaire just isn't what it used to be.

In 1991 it was estimated there were some 500,000 millionaires in the United States. By 2015 that had doubled. In 1940 the number was probably less than 50,000.

The fact is that it takes $20 million or more today just to be equal to being a millionaire in the 1920's, 1930's and 1940's.

To illustrate further say you have $1 million in cash today. You live in a state, like Texas or Florida, with no state income tax. You invest in tax free bonds, at an average yield of 7% (or at least you did before the financial crisis where now you might be lucky to get 3%). Your yearly income is therefore $70,000, after income taxes since you pay none to the state and we assume none to the Federal government or local government as well. Not too bad you say.

But if inflation is running in the future as it has in the past at 5% a year you would need to take $50,000 from that income stream and add it to your capital kitty just to stay even in "real" dollars. If you don't you are fooling yourself about your income because what a $1 would buy you last year will take $1.05 this year. Or put differently your dollar last year is worth only 95 cents this year. Not adding back to your capital what inflation has eroded is like the old farm adage advising you not to eat your seed corn.

That means that our millionaire has a "real" income of only $20,000 a year ($70,000 minus $50,000 for inflation). Not exactly the income you expect of a millionaire. I doubt Robin Leach will be calling you for an appearance on the Rich and Famous. And in the post financial crisis world even though inflation is running less so is the income on tax free bonds so the situation is no different for our poor millionaire.

Is This A Liberal, Anti-Rich Polemic?

Far from it. Unlike the French economist Picketty I do not believe capitalism to be evil. Nor do I believe as some liberals do that salaries of executives should be capped at 10 times worker salaries.

Forgetting the age old arguments over wealth creating jobs, giving incentive to take risk, whether the rich have earned their wealth, there is one argument in favor of the existence of the Super Rich that gets little attention. Yet, while it is valuable it is almost never discussed subject and that is the positive role of the Super Rich in modern society. Oh, and yes the author is far from being Super Rich! Though if enough of you buy this book….

The role I find interesting is the role of symbolizing the brass ring that everyone wishes they could reach. The Super Rich represent the fantasy that many have that one day, with skill, hard work or maybe just plain dumb luck, we or our kids may make it to the point where to continue working is a matter of choice not necessity.

Fantasy? Maybe but it is interesting to look over the Forbes annual 400 list of richest people in America and see the people who have made it there due to their skill.

Sam Walton, and now his family, tops the list. He typified hard, smart work. He didn't stumble over a gold mine, happen to buy a piece of land over a pool of oil or inherit his wealth. In the very short span of 25 years he built a business in the most unlikely of places – rural and semi-rural America. And he did it in one of the toughest businesses there is – retailing. He even forced what was once the largest retailer – Sears into second, then third and today hardly on the list of major retailers. In the process he became the wealthiest man in American and probably the world. No small feat. In addition he made many of his employees incredibly wealthy as well.

Yes, the American Dream lives on … currently in Bentonville, Arkansas.

In case you think that Mr. Walton is an exception, you will find many others on the Forbes 400 list that built their vast fortunes in the space of their lifetime. With the explosion of technology it is not at all unusual to see those in their 20's and 30's on that list.

Remember these are truly unique individuals, those that made it to the very highest levels of wealth. Many, many more have become Super Rich without reaching the levels of the Forbes 400.

We probably should think of great wealth as the ultimate trophy for a successful business career. Think for a minute of how many athletic teams would compete as vigorously as they do if there were no trophies, no first place awards, just a friendly handshake and a "well done" when the game was over. Indeed, if winning and losing is not important then why keep score? Have you ever played a practice game without keeping score? Not nearly as much fun and usually ends fairly quickly.

Armed forces from the beginning of time have known the motivational secrets of awards and rankings. They have handed out medals and awards, ranks and privileges to their best and most courageous to provide incentive and recognition. The Congressional Medal of Honor is awarded today to those displaying the ultimate in courage and gallantry. Who among us does not honor and respect the courage that has won such an award. Not many. And there are high civilian awards too such as the Medal of Freedom or the Nobel prizes.

Goals and honors, from the Pulitzer to the Nobel Prize have many a writer and scientists late at their desk or lab with the hope or dream of one day receiving these prestigious awards and the acclaim that goes with them.

Indeed, what is that keeps a multi-billionaire working late into the night? Greed? Ego? Maybe, but I suspect that they enjoy what they do, that the wealth hasn't been an end in itself but rather the result of the fulfillment of the dream that they had for the enterprise when they started and built it.

It is sometimes disturbing to see athletes and rock stars paid millions for what is in reality rather trivial work. While at the same time our best scientists, teachers and other workers spend their entire lives in contribution to society often for less than the pay for one round of a heavy weight fight or a single event or record of a rock group. Just maybe that is part of the price we pay to keep dreams alive.

I am not a fan of lotteries or gambling in any form for that matter. Yet I recognize that the $1 a week paid by the shoeshine man in my barber shop for a lottery ticket has bought him more than just a lottery ticket. He bought a piece of a dream. Maybe, just maybe, this week will be his lucky one! The one that puts him on easy street. I, for one, find it hard to take away people's little dreams and the happiness they bring in everyday life even though I know the odds against them are enormous.

So I am not opposed to or wish to take anything away from the Super Rich who have earned their wealth honestly. They serve a valuable role in our society and economy.

Besides, if you took every dime of wealth the Super Rich have and redistributed it among every man, woman and child on earth, each probably would receive a check for less than $500. With the symbols and personification of wealth and the easy life gone, so to the dreams would be gone, the incentive to work and strive and to succeed. The hope for the brass ring would have been destroyed forever.

Picking on the rich as the cause of our troubles is, and probably always will be, a favorite game of some politicians but it is a phony game. Our problems are not because some people are rich.

This Book Is Not For The Super Rich

The point of discussing and defining the Super Rich is to point out that the present system works reasonably well for them. They can cope with Congress and their state and local political bodies.

Through their CPA's and tax lawyers and various lobbies, they can stay somewhat ahead of the game. What's more they are the life blood of the present political system. They are the ones who finance the political campaigns, attend the $1000 a plate dinners, who can afford to run for office (a good part of the U.S. Senate would qualify as among the Super Rich) and to serve as senior government officials.

41

Though they probably would not agree, the current political system is fraught with dangers for them as well as for the rest of us. The current "inside the beltway" mentality seems increasingly unreal to many Americans. The myopic view of the world such limited vision produces could be greatly expanded if men and women representing the middle class were heard more often on Capitol Hill.

When this book was first written in 1991 there had been a recent fiasco over the 50% pay raise that Congress voted for itself. It was an example of a political system out of touch with the average American. The pay raise was recommended by a panel of the Super Rich – to whom the raise seemed a pittance. And those who know Washington and its expenses know that then current salaries did not permit a reasonable standard of living in the Capital. But the average American does not live in Washington DC and does not understand. There's the rub. Congress, and its patrons, the Super Rich, are not in touch with the economic reality facing most Americans. Occasionally the silent majority (as Richard Nixon used to call them) will rise up and tell them so. Unfortunately not often enough. Oh, and do you remember what happened to that pay raise? It was nixed, but only until they could quietly slip it in when few were watching.

And What Of The Poor?

There has always been a fear of those in power of the masses. The Romans gave their masses the circus to keep them happy. In the middle ages kings sent their masses following troubling nobles on crusades to keep them out of the way. In the 1960's riots in Watts, Harlem and Miami brought out cold sweat on the brow of political leaders. And more recently events in Ferguson, MO and Baltimore, MD show that risks continue with political leaders fanning the flames, modern Neros.

After all, the lessons of the French and Russian revolutions, when the disenfranchised and poor rose up against their leaders, is a bloody bookmark in any leader's history book. A bookmark to be misplaced only at one's peril. Ask the former leaders of Eastern Europe after the fall of the Soviet Union.

A combination of fear, or at least unease, plus a measure of guilt and a small amount of genuine compassion, will generally lead to programs to keep the masses at bay, or in current political lingo, to provide them an economic safety net. Whatever the motivation the tending to needs of the less fortunate is worthy of any people who call themselves civilized. This is not a polemic against the poor either.

While we do not provide all the services that the poor may need programs do exist and great attention is paid to trying to provide for the most basic needs of those at the bottom of the economic ladder. To illustrate the point that attention is paid to the poor let's do a little test. For a week watch any of the national news programs and your local news. Note how many segments deal with 1) the problems of the poor and how many with the 2) problems of the middle class. My guess is that other than with the possible exception of Fox News you will find far more discussion of the problems of the poor.

Then There Are Those In The Middle

This book was first written in 1991 and back then there was practically no discussion of the disappearing middle class. Recently there has been more focus on the issue. The problem of tending to the needs of the middle class is the stark economic reality that in the United States while there were in 1991 probably fewer than 50,000 Super Rich and about 32,000,000 poor there were some 200,000,000 that were somewhere in between. At that time the middle accounted for nearly 90% of all economic activity. And while in 2016 despite all the problems they face the middle class is still quite large. Unfortunately they have faced stagnating job openings and stagnating incomes. Since the financial crisis of 2008 while those with below high school education have seen their job participation rise to pre-crisis levels that has not been true of those with High School or higher educational degrees. Not only have the jobs not come back (many are working more than one job and doing part time jobs) their income has stagnated or declined.

But despite the decline of the middle class the fact is that the middle class pays for government at all levels. When taxes are needed the burden always falls on the middle. If every dime of income over $200,000 were taxed (as it was in England for many years) at 100% the revenue raised would not pay 10% of the Federal budget for one year, not to mention state and local revenue needs. And corporate income taxes do not help the middle; they merely hide the tax in form of higher prices for products sold. In the end consumers pay corporate taxes in the form of prices for products.

So next time you are watching your favorite evening news show and hear how your favorite Congressman or woman plans to balance the budget by taxing the rich, don't believe it for a minute. The real tax burden will fall where it always has, where it has to, on the middle.

Worst of all is the fact that Congress is only one of the political institutions that can stick their hands in your pocket. States and local tax authorities are routinely tapping more and more of your income. And they are doing so in clever ways, from sin taxes on alcohol and cigarettes, to motel taxes, sales taxes galore, local and state income taxes, property taxes and on and on.

There is no coordination of any of these burdens. Each looks only at its problem, not at your problem. Added up the burden of all these taxes can be staggering.

At the end of the Regan Presidency, U.S. News and World Report did an analysis and one of its findings was that despite the Reagan Federal tax cuts the total tax burden, Federal, state and local increased steadily throughout the Reagan years, up to a total of 40 cents out of every dollar of income in 1988. And it has not gotten better since then. In 1991 it was announced by the Tax Foundation that in that year Americans would work 3 more days to pay their Federal, state and local taxes than the prior year. Thank about that for a minute. In one year, just one year, the effective tax burden increased by almost one full percent. And they think that Chinese water torture or waterboarding is bad. It is nothing compared to the drip, drip, drip of tax dollars leaking from your pocket.

The Major Problem Areas – Education And Health Care

Remembering again that this book was first written in 1991 what are now, some 25 years later, hot button issues were ones just coming on the horizon. Back then the author of this book wrote about these as follows.

Let's look at the two major issues facing most middle income families today – college education and health care.

First, education. The value of a college education is not what it used to be. Before WWII only about 5% of college age kids went on to college. Being a college graduate was a symbol of the highest levels of economic society. Today the percentage of kids going on to college is 25%. (That was in 1991).

In many ways a college degree today is equivalent to what a high school degree was in the 1930's and it costs a whole lot more.

A four year college education in 1991 was costing from $20,000 to $100,000 while in 2016 you can multiple those figures by 4 to $80,000 to $400,000 for private colleges and universities with some public universities perhaps half that cost. What is worse is that the cost is escalating faster than inflation generally while help for the middle class parent and student is declining.

The sad result is that a poor kid or a rich kid of equal or even lower academic standing will end up at a better college than the child of a middle class parent. Reading college brochures will tell you that the child in "need" will generally have 100% of their "need" covered. Not so the child of the middle class.

An article by John Hood reprinted in the Reader's Digest pointed out that:

"The cost of a college education…From 1981 through 1987, it rose 99% faster than median family income and three times as fast as the cost of living."

And since then it has not gotten any better!

He went on to talk about what regrettably has become a common problem in many large scale government programs.

"Student aid has become largely predicated on need, linking the availability of Federal and state subsidies to student's ability to pay. Many colleges have taken the bait and made school more expensive to attend, thus boosting their Federal dole. This, in turn, has fueled political pressure on government to increase its need-based student aid. The result is a vicious circle."

In 2016 there is even talk of making college education free for all no matter their ability or need for that education. And just who will pay for that I wonder!

An excellent article, deeply troubling in its analysis and conclusions is by Jay Amberg in the autumn 1989 issue of The American Scholar entitled, "Higher (-Priced) Education." He concludes: "While the cost of higher education spirals upwards quality…winds down to mediocrity."

To put the issue in proper focus, let's consider two young families. Identical in age, family size and income. Family A spends its income to the maximum, saving very little. Family B saves 10% of its income, sacrificing meals out, vacations and other pleasures that Family A routinely enjoys.

When it comes time for college, Family A has $20,000 in assets, principally in their home equity, while Family B has $200,000. Want to guess which family has the most "need" on the scholarship forms? You guessed it, Family A is the winner. Any wonder that American families do not save like their Japanese counterparts.

Returning for a moment to the Reader's Digest article it is interesting to see the editorial response it received. The Wall Street Journal cited it in discussing what it saw as "rampant waste in

American higher education." And concluded that "An ordinary taxpayer is to be forgiven if he draws the harsh conclusion that in much of higher education nowadays, when it comes to grants and loans the driving force seems to be you get whatever you can while the getting is good."

I would like to tell you that in the 25 years since this was written things have gotten better. In fact they have gotten worse.

So much for the cost of higher education, what now of a second major worry for the middle class, health care? Remembering that this was written before Obamacare the problems remain and the ultimate story of Obamacare has yet to be written. Only now are the cracks and costs of that program beginning to appear and once more there is political talk of a single payer (Canadian or British style socialization of medicine) system. Indeed one can be forgiven for thinking that Obamacare was created in a way to ultimately fail so that the progressive element in our political system could marshal support of the masses for its ultimate dream, the single payer system run by none other than that old leprechaun, Usa.

Working with Families A and B again assume that Family A and Family B parents now reach retirement. Family A again has its $20,000 in assets but lots of pictures of their cruises (financed), their

RV (financed) not to mention their trips to Las Vegas. Family B on the other hand has an IRA of $200,000 and a house paid for, worth $175,000 and stocks and bonds worth $200,000. A grand total of their assets of $575,000.

Family A and B both qualify for Social Security. But good old Family B, because they saved their money, find that 85% of their Social Security is subject to tax. And had the Catastrophic Medical Care system not been repealed they would have had to pay 15% to 25% extra on that tax. Neither one of which would be paid by free spending Family A.

In years since this was first written the situation for Family B has gotten worse. Added Part B premiums for high income families has been introduced as a "fix" for Medicare and added taxes were imposed as part of Obamacare. And why again do Americans not save more?

It would seem that there is a lesson here about the rewards of saving in America. And it is a lesson apparently most Americans have learned. Spend it quick, before Usa can steal it.

By the way if parents of Family A or B ends up in a nursing home, at high expense, guess which one has to sell their assets, give up their home, until they reach the poverty level that will qualify them for

Medicaid? Yes, you guessed right again. The loser is Family B.

Sadly, the prudent, saving family is the loser in a system of "need" based assistance. It seems to this author there is something seriously wrong with a system where we reward the profligate and penalize the prudent.

As for health care in general, a large part of our national budget problem can be traced to health care costs run amuck. Medical costs in 1991 took up 12% of our Gross National Product. Up from only 6% in the 1960's. The World Bank notes that in 2013 this has risen to 17% in 2013 and continues to rise.

The Medicare portion of Social Security is our most serious problem in budget balancing. Unfortunately it may well have been Medicare that put us on this path to begin with. Just as the article and editorial on college costs, cited earlier, point out when you hold out a blank check don't expect the recipient to fill in a small or reasonable amount.

There was a time, not very long ago, when our physicians were honored, as typified by the TV show Marcus Welby, MD. Regrettably Medicare made medicine a profit center and what were once honored professions and hospital charities became big business. Very big business.

In the process the healers have become well-heeled. A student was recently asked what the initials "MD" stand for. He responded without hesitation, "Mercedes Driver."

Unfortunately, while the providers of health services and the administrators of their "charities" may be driving Mercedes or other high end cars, many of their patients are being driven to the bankruptcy courts. Want a real eye opener? Go down to your local bankruptcy court and see how many bankruptcies are the result of unpaid medical bills. You will be shocked.

Again, don't misunderstand me. As far as I am concerned health care providers should be well paid. If they can provide quality care at a reasonable cost, I don't care how much they can make. But when older Americans and even younger Americans are forced into poverty to pay for care and when businesses face year after year of 20-40% increases in insurance premiums for health care and when bankruptcy dockets are filled with medical debtors....all while doctors, hospital administrators, insurance company executives and their cronies are all trying to outdo one another by conspicuous consumption...something is very, very wrong.

And don't buy the malpractice smokescreen. It is a problem for sure, but not the real problem. It is currently the excuse for more and more gouging by doctors, hospitals and insurance companies. "Gee, we didn't want to run all those tests, do all those procedures (for which we collected fat fees) we had to do it to avoid malpractice. The lawyers made us do it! If it made us rich in the process well, I guess we will just have to live with it. See you in Aspen!"

Back in the 1990's the Wall Street Journal ran a story saying that medical costs for the next year were going up by 20% on top of the 25% increases the year prior. Yet less than 1% of the increase was due to increases in malpractice costs. It seems to me that they "doth protesth too much"…and pocketeth to much as well.

I do want to be clear on one point. I have great respect for the truly dedicated physician. I am fortunate to count a few as my friends. Regrettably, even some of these have become caught up in the politics of their profession. Those who seek mammon over medicine make it incredibly difficult for those who do not share in their greed. Even our advertisers have picked up on the theme. An ad for breath mints once showed a mother urging her marriage age daughter to chew quickly a mint because she has invited an eligible young doctor to dinner. Many parents want their children to become or to marry doctors, not because it is an honorable profession with compassion for the sick but because it is the ticket to riches and the good life.

One of the jokes going around goes like this. "What is the difference between the Italian Mafia and the Medical Mafia? The answer is the Italian Mafia gives you a choice – your money *or* your life."

Many of us know of cases where patients were given the finest quality care…right up to their last dollar. Saddest is the truly dedicated doctor, nurse or health care professional who still upholds the traditions of an honorable profession. Their voices and concerns are often lost in the language of the business of modern medicine.

Again it is the middle class that suffers the most from the health care crisis. While there are programs for the poor and none needed for the very wealthy, the vast majority in the middle is frozen out or suffers an increasingly large share of its income siphoned off for health services. We are approaching 25% of Gross Domestic Product spent on health care and with no end in sight.

Is it any wonder then that those in the middle feel increasingly frustrated? Feel they are on a treadmill that seems to take them one and a half steps back for every step they try to take forward?

It is my basic thesis that the current political system focuses on the top and bottom of the economic ladder while the silent middle pays and receives altogether too little attention in the process. College and health care costs illustrate this only too painfully. As does child care for increasingly single parent families. It is a focus that needs more than political stump lip service that it gets today. We need less talk about the decline of the middle class and more action.

The Story of the Three Legged Pig

The plight of the middle class reminds me of the story of the farmer with the three legged pig.

It seems a salesman stopped one day at a farmer's house and was talking to the farmer. All the while the farmer was holding a young pig with a pretty ribbon tied to its neck, but with only three legs.

Unable to still his curiosity, the salesman finally asked the farmer why the pig only had three legs.

"Well," the farmer said, "This is a really fine pig. Just last week I was in the south forty when this little fellow came running to me squealing. I followed him back to the house and found it on fire with my young daughter inside. This little pig leapt from my arms and ran into the house and led her to safety while I put out the fire."

"That is truly remarkable!" exclaimed the salesman. "But you still haven't told me why it has only three legs."

"Well, sir, let me tell you another thing about this pig." Said the farmer. "Week before last my tractor turned over on top of me and had me pinned underneath. It was this little fellow that ran for help and saved my life."

"Unbelievable," marveled the salesman "That truly is a remarkable pig, but you still haven't told me why it has only three legs."

"You see it is this way, "said the farmer slowly "when you have a pig this good...you just don't eat it all at once."

Like the poor little pig, those in the middle don't get eaten all at once, just a bite hear and a nibble there. One day the farmer (Congressperson or bureaucrat) may find they have taken one bite too many and lo and behold...there is no pork left in the barrel!

Chapter 4 Statesmanship and other lost arts

I considered omitting this chapter. As I thought about the state of statesmanship today it seemed unlikely I could make a full chapter on the subject. That, it seems to me on further reflection, is the whole problem.

It was not that long ago that there were statesmen (and it was mostly men because women were not part of the process to the extent they are today) on the national and world scene. Men of reason and wisdom, who by force of their wit and tongue and perspicacity, were able to fire imagination and to lead people and nations in what they viewed as proper paths to follow.

Winston Churchill, probably the greatest of modern statesmen, stands tall when compared to current leaders. So too statesmen from our past, men like Daniel Webster, Ben Franklin, Lincoln. Men like Teddy Roosevelt, Woodrow Wilson, and Franklin Roosevelt. Then there are those unelected statesmen such as the humorist from Claremore, Oklahoma – Will Rogers or from an earlier time Mark Twain. Whether you agreed with their particular vision they had that elusive capacity to lead, to mold your thinking in new paths.

It is hard today to name a modern figure one would clearly call a "statesman" in the league of those mentioned above. Maybe we are too close to them, or maybe the modern political process is not producing them. Probably Margaret Thatcher comes closest and many would include Ronald Reagan. President Obama had the chance at becoming a statesman but sadly has tended to fan the flames of racial tension rather than calming those troubled waters as one hoped at the start of his Presidency. Compared to leaders of the past he appears very much an empty suit.

Let's play a game to illustrate the point further. Take pen and paper. Now write down three memorable quotes from a current U.S. Senator. Now do the same for a current U.S. Congressman or woman. How about your state Governor? Your local Senator or State legislator.

I am willing to bet that you still have a blank sheet of paper. I know I did when I tried. I could come up with lots of memorable and meaningful quotes from past statesmen, but the last senatorial quote I thought of was long gone Senator Everett Dirkson's quip … filled with considerable insight I might add…that you take " a billion here and a billion there and pretty soon you are talking about real money." A quote from his commentary on government waste and extravagance.

With all our modern technology, truly marvels of scientific and industrial achievement, we seem to have moved backward in our ability to govern based on more than knee-jerk reactions to one crisis or another. In a democracy, consistent policies require genuine statesmanship to craft.

Churchill accomplished such a feat with his famous "Iron Curtain" speech at Westminster College in Fulton, Missouri after World War II. In this speech he reminded the world of the legacy of those who did not admit the danger they faced who consequently failed to prevent what could have been prevented. In the case of the Iron Curtain, Churchill created a clear, almost visual, idea with which statesmen and common men and women alike could relate. He marshaled the Western world to stop what then appeared to be a march of the Russian empire from the Urals to the coast of France. Who among us can fail to have been moved deeply the events of recent years in Eastern Europe as the Iron Curtain rusted and crumbled. And despite the efforts to turn the tide by President Putin he has far from regained the lost Soviet Empire. At least not yet.

Churchill knew too well the perils that faced those who did not face reality. After all, it fell to him to clean up after Neville Chamberlain and his well-meaning, but wrong thinking, colleagues refused to face the reality of Nazi Germany until it was too late. The debates in our own Congress (one of its finer moments in recent years) over the Gulf War was all too reminiscent of the debates that ranged across Europe before the world was plunged into the abyss of World War II. And it is too early yet to tell the outcome of the Middle East crisis ranging from ISIS to Iran complicated by plunging oil prices in 2015-16.

I fear that the modern political process brings us more good lookers than good thinkers, at all levels. Those who fail to look good for TV, speak in monosyllabic "sound bites" such as "read my lips, no new taxes!" and resolve complex problems in sitcom speed, do not stand much of a chance today in the polling booth. And whether you like or dislike Donald Trump on the campaign trail he is merely the creation of the modern TV media. A showman is rewarded while the statesman is retired.

The pace required of election campaigns, not to mention the pace for fund raising, leaves little time for reflection on the problems of the world. The computer and copy machines produce volumes of studies, reports and papers that even the most dedicated speed reader could never hope to devour, much less absorb. Who can forget Congresswoman Pelosi and her comment on Obamacare that, "we have to pass the bill so that you can find out what is in it," Act first, think later.

It seems to me we need to seek a way to develop statesmen and women for the development of policies and programs that will move us as far forward in the social sciences as we have moved in the natural sciences.

Our deliberative bodies must become truly deliberative. If you have ever watched a session of C-Span coverage of Congress where one lone Senator or Congressperson is speaking to an empty chamber, it leaves you with a sense of deep despair. Is this the state of 21st Century statesmanship? Voices speaking to absent ears? Even when there is a full chamber and a serious debate member after member rises to reserve his or her right to correct and expand upon their remarks…which means that their staff will stuff the Congressional Record with page after page of commentary that few will ever see and fewer more care about. It is all too reminiscent of the old philosophical argument about whether a falling tree in the forest makes a sound where there is no one there to hear it. Or perhaps the wag who told us that, "Those that love the law and sausage should never watch either one being made."

Return Of The Statesman and Woman

There was a day in our system when those in public service saw it as their obligation to look after not only the majority but the minority. I am speaking of far more than the interests of racial or ethnic or geographic or sexual minority interests.

Take an example the enacted and deenacted Catastrophic Health Care program. Aptly named I might add, though with certain retrospective irony! To finance the program Congress imposed 15 to 25% surtax on senior citizen's income taxes. Protests were vigorous. Amazingly the protests were successful. Amazing because seniors are still a minority of the population. Because it is only a minority of this minority that would have paid the tax, had it been allowed to stand, they made for easy prey. Remember that three legged pig.

I saw one report where a poll was taken of seniors and found that a majority approved the new tax. Of course they did! Why would not 2/3 of the seniors who stand to benefit object to taxing the other 1/3d? Put to a vote, of course the 2/3 would vote to take it from the 1/3 minority. You can take that to the bank.

What Congress didn't consider was that the group they chose to pick on this time were some of the more active and articulate politically. They formed letter writing teams, visited their representatives and generally made life miserable for them until they relented.

Such an effort should never have been needed. Congress should have acted in a statesmanlike manner to protect the 1/3 minority. After all what message does this send? To me it said that those who save for their old age will be readily sacrificed for the benefit of those who didn't. Remember the Romney 47% comment that did as much to torpedo his candidacy as anything?

As with all the recent penalties on those who were prudent, who saved and invested, the message is clear…spend it quick, before they can steal it from you! The morality of the current Congress is simple – if you have it, we want it. So hand it over. Seems to me Jesse James had a similar philosophy. Where oh where is Pinkerton and his trusty men when we really need them.

It is a bit like the farmer sitting lazily under the shade tree while his neighbor sweats in the sun to plant his crops. Then, when the crop comes in the lazy farmer gets up and helps himself to part of the harvest. After all, he reasons, he needs it as much or more than the farmer who planted it.

Chapter 5 The paper and electronic avalanche and moral imperatives.

Scott's Law of Morality

Sitting in a law library, surrounded by millions of pages devoted to the laws of the land, facing the hundreds of volumes of new laws generated each year, I feel that there is a rule about law and morality that needs to be stated:

SCOTT'S LAW:

THERE IS AN INVERSE RELATIONSHIP BETWEEN THE LENGTH OF A LAW AND COMPLIANCE WITH THAT LAW.

Simply stated, the more complicated the law the less likely people will obey it.

Moses knew about Scott's Law thousands of years back in time. He gave his people ten simple, straight forward commandments. No chapters, subchapters, sections, subsections, sub-subsections, interpretative regulations, technical corrections, etc. etc.

It is my feeling that most people want to obey the law. But there is no possible way today that anyone can have more than the most basic sense of what the law requires of them.

Take the Federal tax code. To paraphrase the comedian Henry Youngman commenting on his wife he said "take my wife ....PLEASE!" I feel the same about the Internal Revenue Code. The basic Internal Revenue Code alone runs to well over 2400 pages and its basic regulations over 4800 more pages and that was in 1991! Believe me it has not shrunk in these last 25 years.

There was a recent argument after a candidate claimed that the code ran to 80,000 pages and was ridiculed as a result. Analysis indicated there were 3.5 million words and in a standard Word format page that would only come to 11,000 pages! Of course forgetting complexity of reading if you could read at 300 wpm it would only take you 2000 hours to read the basic code. Doubtful you would understand it but that is how long it would take to read it at a very fast reading speed. But they say that if you strip out the indexes it comes to only 5,000 pages! That is up more than 100% in size in just the last 25 years. And Obamacare has just made even the simplest of taxpayer's annual chore even more complex provided they have to buy their own insurance.

The trade press makes an annual event out of taking hypothetical tax facts to the IRS and to tax preparers and reporting on the results. One Money magazine story reported it received right answers from the IRS only 41% of the time. They took this same mythical tax family information to 50 different preparers and… you guessed it… came up with 50 different results. And that was back in the 1990's without Obamacare and other Obamanations in the tax code to deal with.

That report would be humorous but for the fact that taxes are no joke for those caught in the middle of the economic ladder. A similar result was reached by the government's own General Accounting Office.

The result is that the lawmakers have pompously and callously made criminals of an entire nation! No one can escape a microscopic analysis and be found to have obeyed every law of the land. It only takes a pernicious prosecutor to root around and find laws that were likely in all innocence broken to go after the putative offender.

What does this do to the morality of the average citizen? You can bet with assurance that it makes them more cynical, uneasy and less law abiding.

I once saw a piece detailing the personnel policy manual given to new employees of Nordstrom's, a Western US department store chain. As between the company and its employees these rules have the effect of law. The manual stated only two rules for employee conduct regarding customers.

Rule One: Use your good judgment
Rule Two: There are no other rules

To me this made a lot of sense. Moses like in its simplicity but emphasizing what is really important and that is the use of good judgment dealing with customers.

While I have paraphrased what I recall of this policy statement, this is the basic common sense of it. Such trust and common sense may have a direct bearing on why Nordstrom's has been so successful.

Nordstrom's has distilled Scott's Law to its barest essentials. It tells employees that they have been hired on the assumption that they know how to treat people. That the extremity sticking up from their collar can serve a purpose beyond that of a hat rack. That they have the ability, and indeed an obligation, to use their common sense and judgment to see that customers are satisfied and the business runs smoothly.

The frustration with complexity has led many states to enact "Plain English" laws regarding consumer contracts, requiring that they be written so they can be understood. Not sure if these days there is a "Plain Spanish" version. Regrettably no such law seems to govern the lawmakers themselves!

I have often thought it would be salutary to require that all laws in a jurisdiction expire each year and that a single, arthritic, slow writing scribe be required to hand write the laws that will continue to the next year. I had thought of requiring them to be chiseled in stone, to slow the process further, but on further reflection I did not want them to become that permanent.

Cornell publishes on line texts of the Internal Revenue Code and I invite you to peruse some the sections to see the kind of gobbledygook laws you and I are required, under penalty of law, to obey. Read and enjoy…enjoy a good cry that is.

Here is the link:
https://www.law.cornell.edu/uscode/text/26

Perhaps the best news science has brought us in recent years is the discovery that all paper is not acid free and that paper that is not acid free will disintegrate in a few years. Now all we need to discover is how to accelerate the process. When I first started in business one of the early copy processes was called Thermofax. The paper produced would harden and crumble into dust in about a year. Alas progress has brought us more durable copies in the years since. I am not at all sure this is real progress at all.

If we are to put our national morality on a sound footing then we must return our lawmaking to an understandable and sound footing. We start by disciplining the process, requiring that laws be enacted in a form that can be understood and obeyed by the average person against whom they are to be enforced.

It is interesting and instructive to note that the English legal system existed for many years on the barest of written laws, relying instead on the common law system. Without getting into an arcane discussion of comparative legal systems, the heart of the common law system was reliance on the good judgment and common sense of those trained and entrusted to be the guardians of the law. Engrafted on that system was the jury by which the common sense of the peers of the community could be brought to bear on a particular case.

Until we can again inject common sense and reason into our lawmaking process we will continue to weaken the moral fiber of our society.

Indeed the entire future of the Union of States may depend on our success in redressing the current system. Is the United States immune from the forces of disintegration that are infecting other large nations from Canada (Quebec) to the former Soviet Union and the splintering of former Soviet republics. Is it not conceivable that someday the

Western United States, heavily Spanish in ethnicity may tire of Washington and decide they would rather go it alone? After all California is the sixth largest economy in the world all by itself. And other regions may find that their regionality has more bearing on their economic and social welfare than remaining a part of an increasingly polyglot republic. Interesting and not a little frightening to contemplate. The South may yet rise again! And the West, and the Southwest and perhaps the Midwest. Impossible you say…I am not so sure.

Before we leave this subject another example will serve to illustrate the point. The U.S. Constitution is a document remarkably short and to the point. Compare it to most of our State Constitutions which drag on for page after page after page. While the U.S. Constitution has been interpreted and reinterpreted over the years the fundamental principles stand sharp and clear in the minds of most citizens. Can we say the same for our State Constitutions?

If we can ever return statesmanship to the process and common sense to lawmaking perhaps we can reverse the trend to ever increasing complexity. I am persuaded that our survival as a civilized republican democracy demands it. Until then all we can do is try to find ways of dealing with the every changing madhouse on the Potomac. Our next chapter will discuss some basic survival skills needed in surviving the Congressional obstacle course.

Chapter 6 How to Survive the Madhouse on the Potomac

Recognizing the problem that Congress and the Federal bureaucracy presents is one thing; finding out how to live with it is another. A few basic survival skills may help.

RULE ONE: KEEP ALERT AND INFORMED

The foremost defense is constantly to keep informed on how the wind is blowing along the Potomac. Being able to sense change and direction is essential. As is a keen sense of the cycles of political policymaking.

One who wishes not to be run over by a truck had best cross the road only after looking carefully both directions…and then run like hell to get across! The same applies in not being run over by Congress.

There are more than a few publications that can help you keep an eye on developments. Trade groups of all stripes exist on a constant stream of information on the Washington scene.

Yet it is vital to separate fact from propaganda. Often bills are presented that everyone knows are doomed but which give the presenter, with a straight face of course, the opportunity to say he gave it his all….check please. And this allows the trade group that worked with him the chance to say they gave their all…check please.

Unfortunately it is only from experience (I hope not too painfully acquired) that you can begin to separate the genuine forecaster from the political astrologer.

Obviously the first line of defense is a good general news magazine. Then there are the long established newsletters like the Kiplinger Washington Letter and Kiplinger Tax Letter. Often these will give you some advance warning of changes that will affect you.

One example was the handling by Congress of the Single Premium Life Insurance Policy. Around for many years it picked up popularity after the passage of the 1986 Tax Reform Act. For those not familiar with the product in essence you paid one lump sum premium when you obtained the policy. They then wrote the smallest life insurance policy they could and still have it treated as life insurance. The balance of the money was then treated as an investment with rates of return that changed each year. You could borrow the amount you invested and the accumulated income whenever you wanted. Repayment could be deferred to your death. Since earnings on life insurance were not taxed currently this meant that just like in an IRA, earnings built up tax free. Unlike an IRA, there was no limit on the investment and you could withdraw your investment and earnings tax free at any time simply by borrowing it from the account. Various policies had variations on the theme but this was the main idea.

A tax free savings account meant lots of lost revenue for Usa. As long as the product was not widely distributed nothing was done. When insurance companies and agents started really promoting and selling the product Congress took action. The 1986 Tax Act took away most of the benefits. But for once at least they did so only for future policies.

To anyone paying attention the result was clear a couple of years in advance although exactly how Congress would deal with the problem was not. By keeping informed you could have benefited from the confusion and kept yourself at the smallest risk.

Sometimes you are not so lucky. The Tax Reform Act of 1986 is a classic case. Remembering that this book was written in 1991 at that time this Act was fresh in my mind. But it was also one of the last times that a major overhaul of the Tax Code was enacted. True the Bush years made a lot of changes from eliminating the estate tax (for a while until a new administration reinstated it) and Obamacare has made even more changes. But the

Tax Act of 1986 stands alone in the number of major changes in rules long in effect. At the time no one really gave it a chance of passage. It caught most experts in the field flat footed. There was no time for most people to adjust and only fast action after the fact could contain the damage to many people's planning.

RULE TWO: ACT QUICKLY

Whenever change is coming that will affect you it is essential to act quickly once you are certain of the outcome.

The Tax Reform Act of 1986 again contains many examples where the nimble benefited. For example, with the change in capital gains tax the quick acting were able to take advantage of the lower rates for the few months at the end of 1986 while those who procrastinated ended up with higher rates in 1987.

Business owners who for years had been sheltering income in the corporations suddenly found their tax world turned upside down. Again, the quick to react were generally able to modify positions to their advantage or at least contain the damage to their positions.

RULE THREE: NEVER PLAN TOO FAR AHEAD

As a corollary to Rule Two requiring quick action there is a rule that cautions not to plan too far in advance. Who would have guessed in 1985 that capital gains would no longer be favorably taxed after 1986 (and in the 1990 Tax Act only mildly favored)? Not many. Who would have guessed that limits on charitable contributions, interest deductions and a host of other changes, discussed and rejected for decades, would really be enacted into law. Again, not many.

Those who planned too far ahead relying on Congress not to change the rules on them were in for a very rude awakening.

It used to be a rule among conservative tax practitioners never to consider the tax effect of an investment until you were sure that the investment made sense without favorable tax treatment. Those who truly followed this rule were amply rewarded when the tax rules changed.

Or how about a student planning his or her college education who suddenly found the rules on student aid and taxation of their scholarships and their summer employment drastically changed.

We have already discussed at length the plight of the retiree who found the rules changed time and time again on his or her retirement nest egg. Lo the poor retiree who planned to far ahead.

It is a wise person who never relies in their planning on any Usa program. Sad to say but those who have counted on these programs have often regretted that they did so.

RULE FOUR: DIVERSIFY

When you do have a Federal program you are relying on it behooves you to study carefully and think about what changes could be made. Then try not to rely solely on Usa or any one program.

It was interesting in the wake of the financial crisis to see all the ads on TV business programs promoting gold. Forgetting that the price of gold never has yet reached the heights claimed for it and has been a poor investment for years now. And those promoting this investment to protect against a highly inflationary government or a government in crisis seem to have forgotten that in the Great Depression gold owned by individuals was confiscated by Usa in exchange for paper money. And foreign investments might have seemed attractive until you look at history and see that in periods when these might be helpful that exchange controls have been implemented upsetting that apple cart.

Take Social Security for example. As a young man in the 1960's I remember reviewing the benefits my family would have if something cut my life expectancy short. I started with survivor's benefits under Social Security, my life insurance, etc.

Fortunately I did not put much weight on Social Security benefits. I suspected even then that as the Baby Boom bulge from post WWII hit the system that Congress would change the rules. Never did I dream in my wildest nightmare just how much they would change them. Imagine the family that relied on those benefits to fill the holes in their financial planning.

Putting all your eggs in one basket is always a dangerous strategy. It is especially dangerous when dealing with Congress or their henchmen in the Federal bureaucracy.

AN EXAMPLE OF THE "OPPS, SORRY ABOUT THAT" MENTALITY

An example of how the best laid plans can go awry illustrates the point of not relying on any Federal program or rule.

A manufacturer of fireplaces was keeping a wary eye on the Environmental Protection Agency (EPA) that in turn was considering regulations under the Clean Air Act to control pollutants from wood stoves. Oregon and then Colorado had already acted since their states were most affected.

When EPA finally announced its "proposed" regulations they exempted many wood burning devices. Most of the exemptions were based on sound policy decisions.

Reading the rules the manufacturer found that it was fully exempt because its appliance was a furnace providing whole house heat and was coded as such by all three major building code groups.

Then one day the manufacturer opened his mail and found from the EPA a copy of their final rules, effective in less than three months.

Reading the "final" rules the manufacturer found, to his horror, that the EPA had changed the definition of a "furnace" to exclude any appliance that was "located within a living area". Now it is hard to see how a furnace located in a living area causes more or less pollution in the atmosphere than a furnace located anywhere else. However since this manufacturer made a product that is usually located in a living area it is no longer exempt under the exemption it had relied on for nearly a year.

When the EPS was contacted its first response was that the manufacturer should have objected to the proposed rule. Really? Objected to a rule that was just fine with it. No matter that the proposed rule made sense and was just fine as it was!

Because the change was made when it was too late for the manufacturer relying on the proposed rule to do anything about it was just none of their concern. Better luck next time.

A complaint to the manufacturer's Congressman, Small Business Administration and anyone else that would listen was to no avail. You should never have relied on the EPA not to unfairly change its mind.

Fortunately there was a happy ending. Review of the rules showed that another exemption applied and after shelling out thousands of dollars to do quick testing under the exemption, EPA agreed that the fireplace furnace was exempt under that rule.

Incredibly, the EPA formal response ultimately was that they had simply thought about it further and without any public notice had made the unilateral decision to change the rule. While legal remedies were probably available to the manufacturer he and his employees would likely have been long out of business before any court could have come to his aid.

This is one of the more bizarre examples that I have heard about illustrating just how changes in the rules can be carried out with no regard for those who reasonably relied on the rules then in effect.

The callous disregard by Congress and our Federal bureaucracy of the effect of their rule changes on those who reasonably relied on them is a lesson to be ignored only at your greatest peril.

A FINAL THOUGHT

As this last example shows even keeping a close eye and not relying on existing rules and being prepared to act quickly may not save you from a capricious act of Congress or the agencies they create.

Only when the process of government has been altered to consider those who have reasonably relied on existing rules and laws will you be able to safely plan for your future. Until then your only protection is to watch very carefully those who are in a position to affect your vital interests.

My argument with Congress is not that they make changes or even correct mistakes. That is the political process. And it is messy at times. What I do fault in our Congress is the callous way that they treat people who reasonably relied on existing laws and their profligate spending favoring those who vote for a living rather than working for a living. It is not that I do not have compassion for those less fortunate. Quite the contrary. But sadly Mitt Romney was more right than most would admit.

That the 47% who rely on the largess of the Federal government (whether legitimately or not) will tend to cast their votes for those who, like the Romans in the Coliseum, wait for the paternal hand out of bread and other goodies aimed back then at keeping the masses under control and today to acquire their votes. There is more than one way to buy a vote in our current system.

Chapter 7 A Modest Proposal …or two …or five!

I have offered you six chapters on problems that exist in Washington. It is incumbent on me to offer a few proposals that might improve the situation.

Since the problem is one of attitude and attention to the needs of the middle class in particular the changes I propose are designed to produce a new way of governing. Recognizing that no change will be easy (much less politically possible) it is still worth considering what might be done.

PROPOSAL 1: ENACT A CONSTITUTIONAL AMENDMENT PROVIDING THAT ANY SENATOR OR CONGRESSPERSON AFTER THEIR FIRST TERM BE REQUIRED TO OBTAIN OVER 60% OF THE VOTE IN THEIR PRIMARY AND GENERAL ELECTION TO BE REELECTED. THE PERCENTAGE TO BE INCREASED TO 65% FOR A THIRD TERM AND 75% FOR TERMS BEYOND THREE.

The only way this proposal could ever be accomplished would be by way of a Constitutional Convention called by the states. Congress would never in a million years agree to such a change itself.

Of course it is perhaps possible for this change to be implemented for primary elections without a Constitutional Amendment and that is something that the States should consider.

The purpose of this change is to blunt the current incumbent advantage. Term limits have not worked, this might. It is a fact that 98% of incumbent Senators and Congressmen and women are reelected. Because of the advantages of office, the name recognition and perhaps even some good works the incumbent has an almost unbeatable position. And money for reelection pours mostly into the coffers of the incumbent. Only if they shoot themselves in the foot, or are on the wrong side of a Presidential year tidal wave, will he or she be swept from office. Do they ever know it!

If we are to elect true statesmen and women to office the process must allow for change. Term limits have been tried but have been mostly ineffective. In fact probably more good men and women have exited as they have honored the term limits than have bad apples been thrown out. The reason that I favor the higher vote requirement is that I question not only the effectiveness but the wisdom of term limitation. Bad enough that we have a lame duck President in their second term because of the limit on terms so why add a lame duck Congress. Some say that without reelection pressure the legislator would consider the country and its interests first. Maybe, but with the revolving Washington door they may also consider their outside employment opportunities before the country, not that they would ever admit it. Perhaps more important why should we lose arbitrarily the services of a truly good man or woman?

Making reelection dependent on satisfying an increasingly large portion of the electorate we could accomplish much the same goal as term limits. In addition since they need more and more "minority" votes to be reelected they may realize that protecting minorities as well as majority interests is in their political interest as well.

Also, those who hand out the Political Action Committee (PAC) and other funding must think again about who gets the lion's share of their largess. Now it is the incumbent who gets that share. After all, the Pac-men and women know the odds of reelection and they wisely place their bets accordingly.

By making it much harder to remain in Congress for term after term we should retain the best and replace the rest. At least it is worth thinking about.

PROPOSAL TWO: ESTABLISH A CONGRESSINAL STATEMANSHIP AWARD, TO BE AWARDED EVERY TWO YEARS TO A MAXIMUM OF FIVE FORMER SENATORS,

TEN FORMER CONGRESSPERSONS AND TEN FORMER CIVIL SERVANTS. A MAXIMUM OF 25 AWARDS.

To reward and encourage true statesmanlike behavior a Presidential Commission could be established with twelve year terms, one member appointed each year. This Commission could select and honor retired Senators, Congresspersons and Federal civil servants who displayed true statesmanship and leadership in the performance of their public office.

These awards, designed to be the "Nobel Prize" of domestic politics, would carry mostly prestige. They could be awarded in the off year after each two year Congressional election.

After the first fifty recipients are selected the Commission itself could be appointed from prior prize winners, one from each group in turn (Senators, Congresspersons, Federal civil servants) in succeeding years.

To minimize cronyism on the Commission any Senator or Congressperson selected would have his award confirmed or rejected by a vote of his former constituency. As for Federal civil servants their award could be confirmed or rejected by the Senate.

And the TV gurus would love it! Free programming every two years. In this regard every non-election year would be the best time to hold the award ceremony.

By giving these awards for exceptional service we would be encouraging statesmanlike behavior while spotlighting those who deserve to be honored for their service. Who knows, we might even one day elect a President from among those recognized by their peers and constituents as having done an exceptional job of governing!

PROPOSAL 3: APPOINT A SELECT COMMITTEE FROM THOSE AWARDED THE CONGRESSINAL STATEMANSHIP AWARD TO REVIEW ALL FEDERAL LAWS AND REGULATIONS WITH THE SOLE PURPOSE OF SIMPLIFYING AND REDUCING THEM TO THE MAXIMUM EXTENT POSSIBLE.

To limit the proliferation of laws and regulations each should be subject to a sunset provision expiring after a set period and a commission could be established (preferably from those awarded the Congressional Statesmanship Award) to review and recommend ways to simplify and reduce the volume of laws and regulations to their absolute minimum.

PROPOSAL 4: REPLACE THE CURRENT INCOME TAX SYSTEM WITH A SIMPLIFIED GROSS INCOME TAX.

It is said that the current Internal Revenue Code contains over 200 separate penalties. Every effort to simplify the Code has been a sick joke. Each passing year it changes like a kid's kaleidoscope and it is increasingly clear that no one understands the current law.

The result of this complexity is an unwarranted burden on the taxpayers and a deep feeling of unease and unfairness.

The current Internal Revenue Code is a national disgrace. A patchwork quilt of provisions, it is a trap for the innocent and is riddled with escape hatches for the clever. It only serves the interest of those who make it their field of expertise. We have replaced the alchemists, wizards and soothsayers of old with their modern equivalent – the Federal tax expert.

It amazes me how many cities impose an earnings tax covering only a few lines on a form. One city I lived in even used the back of a postcard for its local earnings tax form. Why then does the Federal government require reams and reams of forms, instructions, etc.? At first the income tax form consisted of four pages. A copy can be found via

89

the   IRS   at   the   following   link:
https://www.irs.gov/pub/irs-utl/1913.pdf

A simple gross income tax, similar to that used by many cities and similar to the original income tax would be workable.

Only those whose interests are served by the incredibly complex Federal tax code would even dare to defend it. Unfortunately that includes the IRS, CPA's, tax attorneys and hosts of special interest groups that have carved a place for themselves in the Code, as well as the Congress whose favors they seek and whose election coffers they fill. It is a national disgrace and while the job will be difficult it needs to be replaced.

PROPOSAL 5: CONSTITUTIONAL
AMENDMENT GIVING LINE ITEM VETO

This is hardly a new proposal. To one not involved in the process the need for the line item veto seems beyond question. Only those with their hand fully extended in the pork barrel can object. Unfortunately that includes most of the pudgy old hands in Congress.

President Reagan on leaving office vowed to carry on his fight for the line item veto. Alas he passed on before this was ever accomplished. The ability of the President to cross out specific items in a particular Congressional district put there to please their constituents is essential if control of the budget process is ever to be achieved.

The fear that a President will use this power high-handedly is worth considering. But then a veto can be overridden and can it be doubted that an abuse of the power would be overridden?

The other proposal of President Reagan was a constitutional amendment mandating a balanced budget. This I do not favor. My reason is that arbitrary controls on budgets just don't work. Generally they create more mischief than they prevent. Creative accountants can always create off balance sheet accounts that make a lopsided budget balance. Remember the Graham-Rudman Balanced Budget Law? Probably not since as well intended as it was it failed to achieve its objective. Rather than an artificial balance we should address the reasons for an unbalanced budget and attack those instead.

IN CONCLUSION

The proposals set out above could go a long way to guiding the ship of state back on a proper course. We should always approach changes of government with greatest of care. Yet we cannot be afraid to set right forms of government that have proven themselves to be harmful to the people and their legitimate interests. I am reminded of the old quip from the long gone POGO comic strip where the cartoon character expounded, "We have met the enemy, and his is US!" I have often wondered if he meant "us" or U.S. or perhaps both.

Until changes are made I leave you with I hope some better understanding why I chose as the title of this book "In God We Trust...Because We Sure Can't Trust Congress!" For those who do place their trust in Congress I can only wish you all the luck in the world...I fear you are going to need it!